HAUS CURIOSITIES

The Power of Civil Servants

About the Contributors

Claire Foster-Gilbert is the founder director of the Westminster Abbey Institute. A current and former member of numerous ethics committees, Dr Foster-Gilbert has played an instrumental role in the medical research ethics field, and has led efforts to shift the Church's thinking on environmental issues.

Peter Hennessy is an independent cross-bench peer and Atlee Professor of Contemporary British History at Queen Mary University of London. Formerly a prominent journalist, Lord Hennessy co-founded the Institute of Contemporary British History in 1986 and entered academia in 1992.

David Normington was a civil servant for 37 years, and served as Permanent Secretary of the Department for Education and Skills (2001–05) and the Home Office (2006–11). After retiring from the Civil Service in 2011, Sir David became the First Civil Service Commissioner and Commissioner for Public Appointments.

Edited and with an Introduction by Claire Foster-Gilbert

THE POWER OF CIVIL SERVANTS

A dialogue between David Normington and Peter Hennessy

First published by Haus Publishing in 2018
4 Cinnamon Row
London SW11 3TW
www.hauspublishing.com

The right of the author to be identified as the author
of this work has been asserted in accordance with
the Copyright, Designs and Patents Act 1988

A CIP catalogue record for this book is
available from the British Library

Print ISBN: 978-1-912208-05-0
Ebook ISBN: 978-1-912208-06-7

Typeset in Garamond by MacGuru Ltd

Printed in Spain

Contents

Acknowledgements

Sincere thanks are due to the Dean and Chapter of Westminster, the Council of Reference and Steering Group of Westminster Abbey Institute, Martin Donnelly, Richard Sargeant, Curtis Juman, Kathleen James, Barbara Schwepcke, Harry Hall, Ruth Cairns, Seán Moore, Sunbeam House in Hastings and Moore's Cottage in Knockanure, County Kerry.

Introduction

In 2015 and 2016 Westminster Abbey Institute held a series of dialogues on the subject of power as it is exercised in the institutions of Government, Parliament, the Judiciary and the media. This little book is based upon the dialogue about the power of civil servants. By way of introduction I will give some context for Westminster Abbey playing host to such a dialogue; describe the place of the Civil Service in the ecology of Government and Parliament; consider some of the challenges and stresses civil servants face; and introduce the dialogue partners, Sir David Normington and Lord Hennessy.

Westminster Abbey sits on the south side of Parliament Square, with the Houses of Parliament to the east, the Treasury and all of Whitehall to the north, and, since 2009 when it moved out of the House of Lords, the Supreme Court to the west. Parliament Square thus consists of the Legislature, the Executive, the Judiciary... and an ancient church. Westminster Abbey may have had a finger in the ruling classes' pies in the past, but these days its proximity to the corridors of power belies any privileged access. Nevertheless, when the idea for Westminster Abbey Institute was proposed in a feasibility study in 2012, it was welcomed by the Abbey's neighbours. Not as another think tank or campaigning organisation, of which there are plenty, and not as an apologist for faith in the public square, but as a place of rest, reflection and challenge to all those who try to run the country. That everything is happening a great deal faster these days is a cliché because it is true, and the pressure on Government and Parliament to respond and decide and deliver speedily, with no quarter given for the unintended consequences of well-intended policies, is intense. It is rare to be given the chance to draw breath and recollect what the policies are really for, to reconnect to one's vocation to public service and the values and virtues that underlie it, and to recharge one's moral batteries thereby. Westminster Abbey Institute tries to provide the means for this refreshment of the souls of the people and institutions so engaged. The series of dialogues on the nature of power was offered in this spirit, as is this book.

Ruling power is located among balancing forces of party politics, Cabinet responsibilities, the Prime Minister's favour, the need to gain and retain votes, the politically impartial support of the Civil Service, public opinion as it is expressed through traditional and social media and 'events, dear boy, events'. To what extent do the different forces support, curtail, outweigh or even completely scupper each other in the shared attempt to express and enact what should be done for the country? The UK constitution puts elected political leaders at its heart and this is where, rightly, responsibility finally rests for the decisions, called policies, that are brought into being. The volatility that is inherent in democracy – as MPs inevitably have to attend to being selected, elected and re-elected – is then given considerable stabilising ballast by the constitutional provision of a non-political Civil Service, Judiciary, Armed Forces and Security Services and an appointed House of Lords, all of whom, together with MPs themselves, owe loyalty first of all to the Crown, which has no direct power at all. The genius of the system is that no one can become a tyrant, but arguably the very same system prevents anything getting done.

'Whitehall' is the public administration that supports the Government in carrying out its task of governing the country. It consists of the home Civil Service and the foreign Civil Service, the latter usually referred to as the Diplomatic Service, divided into 20 or so Government Departments including the Foreign and Commonwealth Office (the Diplomatic Service) and the Home Office, Treasury, Cabinet Office, Department for Environment, Food and Rural Affairs and all the other Departments responsible for domestic policy (the Civil Service). In the UK, Whitehall is politically impartial and civil servants are meritocratically, not politically, appointed, serving with equal loyalty whichever party or coalition of parties has been democratically elected to govern. The particular ethos of Whitehall was proposed as long ago as 1854, when Stafford H. Northcote and C.E. Trevelyan published their *Report on the Organisation of the Permanent Civil Service*.[1] The Northcote–Trevelyan Report states at the outset:

> The great and increasing accumulation of public business, and the consequent pressure upon the Government... and the inconveniences which are inseparable from the frequent changes which take place in the responsible administration... [mean that] it may safely be asserted that, as

matters now stand, the Government of the country could not be carried on without the aid of an efficient body of permanent officers, occupying a position duly subordinate to that of the Ministers who are directly responsible to the Crown and to Parliament, yet possessing sufficient independence, character, ability and experience to be able to advise, assist, and, to some extent, influence, those who are from time to time set over them.[2]

Northcote and Trevelyan candidly observe that nevertheless 'the ablest and most ambitious youth of the country' are *not* attracted to this vital profession. Admission to the Civil Service is sought by 'the unambitious and the indolent or incapable', those who have failed to enter the 'open professions' which are competitive; the result is that 'the public service suffers both in internal efficiency and in public estimation'.[3] The Report insists that appointment to positions in the Civil Service must be on the basis of merit, not patronage, and proposes:

A proper system of examination, for the supply of the public service with a thoroughly efficient class of men; to encourage industry and foster merit, by teaching all public servants to look forward to promotion according to their deserts, and to expect the highest prizes in the service if they can qualify themselves for them.[4]

The Report was published in 1854, but its recommendations were bitterly resisted, including by Queen Victoria, and it took many years for it to be accepted and the meritocratic ethos it proposed to be established. The process was assisted by the creation of the Civil Service Commission in 1855 to ensure senior appointments to the Civil Service were made on merit, a role it maintains to this day. The merit-based, politically impartial Civil Service was thus initiated by the Northcote–Trevelyan Report and remains alive and in reasonable health a century and a half later. Over the ensuing years it has evolved, not least in its admission of women, but also in the honing of its virtues of integrity, honesty, objectivity and impartiality, which have become the DNA of the Service, articulated in the Civil Service Code, which is appended. The virtues exemplify the vision of Gladstone, who made a clear distinction between the public and private sphere, insisting on the importance of a public sphere into which no private interest should intrude.[5] The virtues have, like DNA, replicated themselves with each generation, and were only very recently enshrined in law by means of the 2010 Constitutional Reform and Governance Act to which, in the dialogue, David Normington refers favourably. Principles of impartiality and meritocracy mean that the democratically elected Government of the day is advised by politically neutral, professionally excellent officials whose role is not to be partisan yes-men and yes-women to politicians but to speak truthfully to them on the basis of the best evidence. Officials are also permanent, unlike their temporary political masters, as the Report commends, and so can provide memory and documents to remind Ministers of what worked in the past and why. Moreover, senior civil servants have a shared responsibility to think holistically of Government, not just of their part of it.

Each Government Department has a Secretary of State and several junior Ministers, all appointed directly by the Prime Minister and responsible for the policies of that Department, while the rest of the Department is made up of civil servants who are appointed on merit. In this unique configuration, the leaders of the Government Departments may not appoint their staff, because to do so would render their appointees politically partisan. To some, this seems ridiculous. Where else would you see an organisation in which those in charge have no power of appointment of those serving under them? How could their loyalty be secured? To others, it is a safeguard against too much political (and inherently corrosive) power. Civil servants are obliged to follow the direction set by their Ministers: they have no other masters to serve than lawfulness and propriety, and these should be served by Ministers in any case. Those who question the ability of civil servants to switch allegiance from one party to another with a change of Government have not seen how hard they work beforehand to be ready for such a shift, and how much they are by the very nature of their profession masters of ambiguity, with an uncanny ability to hold apparently conflicting ideas in their minds at one time.

A Government Department is thus rather like a sailing ship, where the direction of travel is set by the Minister but the helming, navigation and all the other tasks of sailing the ship in the chosen direction are carried out by the crew – that is, the civil servants. This includes, of course, sometimes completely redesigning the ship when a Cabinet reshuffle involves shifting policy areas from one Government Department to another. Their tasks include advising the Minister on the wisdom of their choice of direction on the basis of the crew's knowledgeable assessment of circumstances; and they must ensure the ship keeps its place in the fleet of ships of all the Government Departments, especially if the Minister acts like a pirate with his or her own treasure map.

The primary and default requirement on civil servants is to carry out the will of their Minister, and this is the expression and enactment par excellence of the democratic principle. Civil servants are expected to take the governing party's manifesto as the starting point for policy development. If they, and not the politicians, were to determine the policies that govern the country, however able and wise their views might be, technocrats and not democratically elected leaders would be in charge. So, even if the civil servant believes the Minister's idea to be crazy ('courageous' in Whitehall-speak), they may not refuse to carry it out. Practised civil servants will do their utmost to ameliorate bad policy ideas by reference to experience, evidence and reasoned argument, but the outcome will depend upon the personality of the Minister and their willingness to listen. If civil servants believe the policy to be really detrimental to the country and cannot dissuade the Minister, they will ask for a 'letter of direction', which makes it clear that they are acting against their better judgement and only because the Minister has required them to. If relationships between civil servants and their Ministers are good, such a requirement should be a rare occurrence. Even rarer is the resignation of a civil servant, which is the 'nuclear' option when they believe a policy is so wrong that they cannot carry it out under any circumstances.

The underlying structure that carries this unusual degree

of political impartiality is the fact that civil servants, like members of the Armed Forces and the Security Services, owe allegiance to the Crown, not to the Prime Minister. This places them constitutionally in a position of independence, responsible for ensuring the propriety and lawfulness of ministerial decisions. Peter Hennessy reflects on the importance of the notion of Crown service, and David Normington agrees that it might be remembered more explicitly by civil servants, as it is by the Armed Forces and the Security Services, who know very well the value of their political independence and rely upon it operationally.

Government administrations in other countries do not have the same neutrality in the senior roles supporting politicians. In the US, for example, all senior officials are political appointees. There are arguments for this: the official who is outrightly in support of a politician will be emotionally committed to the politician's cause and will believe, like the politician, that their political party is the one that is best for the country. It can be hard for one steeped in political values, believing that one's own political party is the means to achieving good things for the country, to see that another, holding bureaucratic values, believes that 'the good' is achieved precisely by serving whichever party is chosen by the people to achieve that end. By the same token, it can be difficult for the civil servant official who thinks in this cool and impartial way to understand just how strongly and morally motivated Ministers might be to see their party's policies carried out. The values are different, but the intention to serve the good can be the same.

If we believe that non-partisan advice is preferable to

partisan advice, then we will believe that the UK system is the best available. And, given the common propensity to see evidence for our hypotheses wherever we look, a legal requirement to be neutral is not a bad solution to a very human tendency. As Martin Donnelly puts it, advice to Ministers must include 'challenging optimism bias, without allowing that challenge to become an excuse for inaction'.[6]

But the dichotomy between political and bureaucratic values is there, and both politicians and civil servants feel it. Sometimes Ministers need advice on their policies that is attuned to political realities. The advent of the special adviser has been in response to this need. Special advisers *are* appointed by Ministers and are explicitly expected to give advice that takes politics into account. Their role is also encoded in the 2010 Constitutional Reform and Governance Act. At their best, special advisers complement the advice of civil servants, but, as Peter Hennessy and David Normington discuss, they can sometimes clash. Sometimes they start acting like junior Ministers, which can be a problem, not least for real junior Ministers.

Brexit is a stress test of the UK constitution. It is probably the case – though no civil servant will express a view in public on this – that the vast majority of civil servants voted to remain in Europe on Thursday 23rd June, 2016. On Friday 24th June, Whitehall was briefly paralysed by shock and in many cases grief. But by Monday morning the Executive had rolled up its sleeves and started to try and make the policy work the best it could for the country. Clare Moriarty, Permanent Secretary (most senior civil servant) of the Department for Environment, Food and Rural Affairs called together all her thousands of members of staff and agency representatives on that Friday afternoon – both in person in London, and from around the country on the telephone – and encouraged them to 'feel what they needed to feel', but made it clear that they had a job to do now, and their professionalism required that they make a start on it. 'Don't feel too sorry for us,' one Home Office official suggested. 'We came into the Civil Service to put ideas into the best practice we could regardless of what we thought of them. This is just one particularly testing example.' A Cabinet Office official has spoken of managing Brexit in vocational terms. It is his calling, as he sees it, to make Brexit work for the country. Nevertheless, officials have felt, and still feel, the stress of being told to focus on the opportunities rather than the risks of Brexit, when it is the risks that need most handling. The dialogue of this book took place before the referendum, and so David Normington explores these concerns in a postscript which is by turns reassuring, moving and alarming.

Civil servants are, by their nature, diffident and retiring. They do not seek publicity and should not be in the Civil Service if they want to be publicly acknowledged for the specifics of what they have achieved. Their rewards come (or should do) from their Ministers, who know the nature and extent of their work behind the scenes to make policies happen; from the respect and recognition of their peers; from stability of employment, including a level of pay and pension that allows families to live in London; and from general public recognition conferred on them by the honours system. These last two rewards are part of the Northcote–Trevelyan vision of inducements that encourage people of ability to come into and remain in the Civil Service, but the civil servant's role has become, respectively, less stable and remunerated, and less admired.

In recent years, senior civil servants have been stripped of their anonymity through a variety of means, all stemming from a general desire for greater transparency and accountability. The desire is laudable but fulfilling it can be costly, not least because civil servants are not permitted to defend themselves publicly if they are criticised. The Freedom of Information Act 2000, while in principle a means to ensure appropriate transparency, has, David Normington suggests, inadvertently damaged the all-important relationship between Minister and civil servants. Earlier, in 1979, many more Parliamentary Select Committees were created, one for each Government Department, consisting of MPs from all parties. Select Committees are another means of publicly calling a Government Department to account, as they can require any Minister or senior civil servant to appear before them in public and answer their questions.

The most ferocious Select Committee is the Public Accounts Committee (PAC), which examines all aspects of public expenditure. As Peter Waller observes:

> Permanent Secretaries and other senior officials are called regularly. The PAC's hearings are often conducted entirely in a hostile atmosphere, with detailed briefing for its members provided by the National Audit Office. Criticism by the PAC is almost always covered extensively in the press.[7]

Such exposure can be painful, especially as civil servants may not retaliate in the same way as ministers can. The PAC has become distorted structurally because like the other Select Committees it now has an elected chair rather than, as in the past, a former Treasury junior Minister who understood Government finance. This can lead to grandstanding on unpopular policies and put officials in an impossible position. They are speaking in public; they cannot use political arguments with a committee that is supposed to look at implementation.

The PAC serves a critically important purpose, however. The Permanent Secretary is the Accounting Officer for their Department and is by this means directly accountable to Parliament for the 'efficient and proper use of funds'.[8] The PAC's on-record requirement for the rigorous justification of public funds is critical to protecting the Government against financial corruption. Martin Donnelly observes:

> One hundred and fifty years of public service tradition allied to a rigorous system of audit and control through the National Audit Office and Public Accounts Committee together with the personal responsibility of the Accounting Officer, traditionally also the Permanent Secretary, for funds voted by Parliament, give the United Kingdom a system which is the envy of the world in the honest management of public money.[9]

A last-resort expression of accountability takes place through judicial review. This involves a legal challenge to a Government decision, made by a third party (that is to say, anyone can request one). They take place after all the work of policy development has happened and the decision has been made and announced. Hence, civil servants have to have this possibility in mind as they develop the policy ideas of their Ministers and advise accordingly, however irritatingly cautious they appear to be in so doing. They may ask, for example, for a time-consuming public consultation on a policy proposal in order to avoid later challenges.

In recent years there has been a concerted effort to harness the digital revolution in order to make Government more efficient and effective. Technology holds the promise of opportunities to implement policies much more quickly and, if the implementation fails, to discover and deal with failure rapidly and cheaply. Some civil servants are going so far as to suggest that they are no longer policy people but implementation people, with the implication that policy involves unnecessary theorising, when all that needs to be learned about the refinement of a Government service can only be discovered as it is implemented, not before. There is certainly a case for adopting a more open, research-oriented mindset in policy-making, which the formidable digital power of big data and online accessibility can assist, but careful consideration of complex policy options can and should be done within a Department before a service is let loose upon its intended recipients, just as a new healthcare treatment would be tested in a laboratory before it was offered to the patients for whom it was intended.

Whitehall is an intrinsic part of the ecology of Government and Parliament. Its bureaucratic values – values that require it to act as the politically impartial guardian of propriety even as it makes the policy ideas of Ministers work – are different from the political values of Ministers, who will believe that their party's policies are the right ones to bring about the betterment of society. These values express themselves differently, and, at best, complement each other so that really good policies are brought into being and delivered intelligently and well. But for this to happen, the civil servant has to sustain a particular kind of moral tension. As Clare Moriarty puts it:

> Civil servants don't aspire to be politicians. We would be in the wrong job if we did: that much is contained in the fundamental tenet of Civil Service neutrality. So we clearly shouldn't be internalising political value systems – but we effectively have to live by them. The oddity in the civil service 'deal' is not that political values prevail – many leaders have to 'play politics' at some level in order to survive – but that, of everyone in the organisation, only Ministers and their special advisers are expected to subscribe to those values.[10]

There is, then, a fundamental moral tension in the role of the civil servant. But, as David Normington exemplifies, the moral discomfort of being a civil servant is not a sign that something is wrong. On the contrary, its absence could indicate that the civil servant has lost their essential impartiality, which David Normington defends to the hilt. Politicians may grind their teeth at bureaucratic caution, but if civil servants were to become political appointees they could no longer with integrity continue as the guardians of propriety.

Understanding the nature of the moral agency of civil servants is key to understanding the UK's constitution, and through Peter Hennessy's skilful questioning David Normington shows how he embodied this moral agency throughout the many decades of his career in Whitehall.

Dialogue

Sir David Normington, speaker in the dialogue, was most recently First Civil Service Commissioner and Commissioner for Public Appointments, responsible for ensuring that appointments to the Civil Service and to boards of public bodies were on merit after fair and open competition, and for upholding the Civil Service Code principles of integrity, honesty, impartiality and objectivity. Before that, David was a civil servant for 37 years, working in the fields of employment, education and criminal justice. He was Permanent Secretary at the Department for Education and Skills from 2001–05 and at the Home Office from 2006–10. In the latter role he led a Department with over 30,000 staff responsible for policies on immigration, law and order and security, and worked closely with the police service, including the Metropolitan Police, on tackling crime and counterterrorism. In 2014 he chaired an independent review of the Police Federation. He was made a Knight Commander of the Order of the Bath (KCB) in 2005 and was appointed Knight Grand Cross (GCB) in the 2011 New Year's Honours list.

Lord Hennessy, interlocutor in the dialogue, was a journalist for over 20 years with *The Times*, the *Financial Times* and *The Economist*. In 1992 he moved to academia and became Professor of Contemporary British History at Queen Mary and Westfield College, University of London. In both roles he has been expert in unearthing the hidden wiring of the constitution and the power of the machinery of Government in Britain. Widely published and well known as a broadcaster, it is said of Peter that 'in his hands the constitution becomes a breathing, dynamic entity with the power to change history'. He has been showered with awards, honorary degrees and honorary roles in academia and the law, and was created an independent cross-bench peer in 2010.

The text below is a lightly edited version of the dialogue, with additional comments made by David Normington to expand points he made in the original dialogue. These additional comments are enclosed in [square brackets]. He has also written a Brexit postscript, which follows the dialogue.

Peter Hennessy

David, your most recent office as First Civil Service Commissioner was a very great Gladstonian invention. It made you the first and therefore the most venerable of what we now call our regulators. The Commissioner's job, quite simply, is to keep the twin flames of meritocracy and political impartiality alight and alive in the Civil Service. I like to imagine the wraiths, the ghosts, of Sir Charles Trevelyan and Sir Stafford Northcote flitting through your rooms in Great George Street, whenever you and your fellow Commissioners were faced with an appointment that stretched them into the grey areas and might have required the speaking of truth to power. I'm referring to the great Northcote–Trevelyan Report of 1854, which laid down the basis of a politically neutral career Civil Service.

Our discussion will take us widely into notions of public

service and the nature of the Civil Service and its power. And we will enter the deep waters of that fascinating governing marriage between transient Ministers and permanent officials with the valuable but occasionally vexing addition to the governing marriage, the special advisers, adding their own singular recitative.

David, may we start with your own personal formation, if I might put it thus grandly? What drew you to the Civil Service Appointments Board in the early 1970s?

David Normington

In 1973 when I was 21, like my fellow 21-year-olds I was looking for a job. The Civil Service was only one of a number of jobs I applied for – I hadn't had my eye on it from the start; I didn't think of it as a vocation then. But it is true to say that there was a tradition of public service in my family. I had a sense that I wanted to do something worthwhile. But I cannot pretend that at 21 I had a grand plan, it just wasn't like that.

In 1973, applicants to the Civil Service had to pass through three stages of examination and assessment. I failed the first exam, and only got in as the 'fastest loser'. The examiners took the view that they didn't have quite enough candidates who had exceeded the pass mark, so they lowered it sufficiently for me to jump over. Then I got through the second stage. At the final selection board, which we no longer have, I found myself in a room in Whitehall facing seven people around a table. The first question was: 'If you were the Prime Minister and you had to get inflation down, what would you do?' I don't remember what I said, only that my heart was beating fast. But since I'm here to tell the tale I can only presume that my stab at an answer was acceptable.

Peter Hennessy

Tell us more about the public service tradition in your family and how it shaped your thinking. When you graduated in 1973, did you carry in your head a certain idea of what public service was?

David Normington

My father was in Local Government in Leeds and, later, West Yorkshire, so I suppose to some degree the conversations in my family were about the local community and how you could serve it. [My parents certainly did not push me in any direction. But there is no doubt that because of my father's job I had a sense of how public service could improve the wellbeing of a community. I have always tried to bring a sense of place to policy development and I have always enjoyed most the jobs that have taken me out of Whitehall to a school or a community project or a training scheme, to see for myself whether we in Whitehall were having a beneficial impact on the people we were trying to help. When I worked for Charles Clarke as Secretary of State for Education, he gave me for Christmas Tip O'Neill's book *All Politics is Local*, making the point, I think, that policy is only effective if it brings real benefits to people in local communities. The best politicians I worked for never forgot that.] But my family influence is balanced by the impact of Oxford University, where I studied. Oxford had a great tradition of graduates going into the Civil Service, with students encouraged to sit the Civil Service exams almost as a matter of course. Of course that led to arguments later that there were too many Oxbridge graduates at the top of the Service and much effort – rightly – in recent times has gone into widening the intake into the graduate fast stream.

Peter Hennessy
The Civil Service isn't keen to have only Oxford and Cambridge graduates any more, and especially not Classics scholars, though they made up the vast majority of applicants in the 1970s.

David Normington
I read History. [It may be unfashionable to say so now, but studying history at Oxford gave me a great liberal education, opening my mind to different ideas, giving me insights into how people behave and act, honing my skills in assessing evidence and in presenting a case clearly and logically. I also gained a sense of historical perspective, which is invaluable when you are buffeted by the immediate pressures of the day. In retrospect there could not have been a better preparation for working life in the public service.]

Peter Hennessy
That's good; we're quite happy with that. At least I am!

When you joined the Civil Service, did anybody formally teach you public service values? Or were you expected to absorb them through your pores by watching and listening to the older sweats?

David Normington

I think I was supposed to absorb them through my pores. That is not to say that we didn't have excellent training, because we did. More subtly there was this prevailing ethos in which the traditions and values of the Civil Service were simply passed down. That still happens. Inculcating an ethos through example and practice is a good thing, but there's also a danger in assuming that young civil servants simply feel, know and own the values by osmosis without any additional help. [In my view, good induction should always include an explicit discussion of the values of the British Civil Service and why they shape its very nature and being. That becomes even more important as fewer people regard the Civil Service as a lifelong career and more join it later in life from successful careers in other sectors. Some of the greatest failures in recent times have been by those who have entered the Civil Service later in their careers with a different value set and have simply not understood what those four values – integrity, objectivity, honesty and impartiality – really mean. It is very hard to understand from a standing start, particularly after a different career, the need to be nonpartisan and nonpolitical.]

Peter Hennessy

I regret the passing of the Civil Service College. Do you? Do you think we should put it back?

David Normington

I do, yes. Of course, it became the National School for Government and then unfortunately it was wound up. That was a real pity, because I think the National School was established with the ambition to drive the creation of a professional Civil Service abiding by professional values. [In my view, it should have been a powerful force for more effective Government, developing the next generation of leaders and improving professional skills, but always in the context of the fundamental ethos and values of the UK Civil Service. That would, however, have required more civil servants and Ministers to buy into that vision, and a willingness to provide the public funding needed to support the School. Neither of those conditions was fulfilled.]

Peter Hennessy

When you first joined the Department of Employment, now the Department for Work and Pensions, in 1973, it was a time of very considerable industrial strife, not exactly a docile period by any means. Are there any particular individuals in the Civil Service who shaped you in those first years?

David Normington

The Department of Employment was indeed in turmoil, facing industrial relations strife with regular miners' strikes. [Looking back, this really does seem a different age. There was a challenge from the whole trade union movement to the 1971 Industrial Relations Act. Many in the Department I joined felt that democracy itself was under attack. For the first six or seven years of my career in the Department, the prevailing view was that it was impossible to pass trade union legislation or enforce an incomes policy unless there was explicit support from the trades unions.]

As for your question about influences, there isn't any one

person I would single out as an influence on me. [What was interesting about the Department of the time was that it had a strong operational focus and it challenged that stereotype of a rather superior Oxford-educated Civil Service. It was not, for example, situated in Whitehall. There was a strong external focus, born of the fact that Department ran the benefit and employment offices and the Government Training Centres. The senior staff came from many parts of the UK; the soon-to-be Permanent Secretary came from Lancashire. So my induction was not to a 'typical' Whitehall Department but to one that lived in the tough real world of 1973. I think I really benefitted from that, and it has stayed with me.]

Peter Hennessy
We have seen changes in the 'governing marriage' of the relationship between Ministers and civil servants in the 30 years since you joined the Department of Employment, but it's quite hard to see how and when they came about. You have lived through those changes, and although there has been no visible or tangible benchmark of change, they have happened. Can you describe them?

David Normington
'Governing marriage' or partnership is the right term. If I look back over all those years – 42 in fact – I think that in my early days there was more mutual respect and greater trust and confidence between Ministers and senior civil servants. These qualities of the relationship have diminished. The nature of the relationship is never smooth and it will always have its ups and downs. It is always dependent upon the personality

of the Minister in particular. But I think it is right to say that there is a trend towards politicians not trusting civil servants and not respecting them quite so much.

Peter Hennessy
Why do you think that is? The causes are probably multiple.

David Normington
Yes they are. One cause is the 'environment', if I might call it that, of politics and Government. Everything moves much more quickly now and that means there is much less time to reflect and consider. Politicians inevitably want civil servants to deliver their policies more quickly. It isn't in the nature of the civil servant to do something shoddily, which is what they sometimes feel they have to do to meet impossible deadlines. This causes quite some stress, but the Minister is under greater pressure than ever to show that the Government in general, and he or she in particular, has made a difference in a short time.

It's even more important, then, that there are excellent relationships at the top of a Government Department, so Ministers know that their civil servants understand the pressures and want to support their work, but at the same time officials have their own vital contribution to the forming of policy by questioning and reflection, and coming up with the best possible solution. A Department needs a guiding coalition of Ministers, Permanent Secretary and senior civil servants. When it works it is because the relationships are good. But I think the relationships are breaking down a bit, and it's hard to say why.

[This question about the weakening of the 'governing marriage' between civil servants and Ministers is the one I have reflected on most, of all the questions asked by Peter Hennessy. In my career I had excellent relations with most of my Ministers and in my ten years as Permanent Secretary felt that the relationship was close and trusting with most (though not all) of my Secretaries of State. So, my own career provides limited evidence of my assertion that the mutual respect and trust is breaking down.

It is also important to distinguish the normal ups and downs of the relationship from the longer-term trend. There probably always has been – and will be – a degree of mutual incomprehension between politicians, who live and die by the cut and thrust of partisan politics, and civil servants, who keep their political views well hidden and who prefer evidence-based policy to political fixes. One of my Ministers, who actually liked civil servants, referred to us as 'Martians', although I often wondered which of us lived on a different planet. Such incomprehension will always from time to time spill over into frustration that the Civil Service is not sufficiently committed to delivering the political direction in which the Government wants to go.

If you add to this mix the normal problems that arise in any workplace – breakdown in personal relations, incompetence, occasional policy fiascos – then it is inevitable that from time to time Ministers and their Permanent Secretaries will not get on. In such cases the demand will always be that the civil servant, not the Minister, is moved or dismissed. That is in the nature of the 'deal' that the civil servant signs up to.

None of this is evidence of a long-term trend. But I remain

of the view, which I expressed in the dialogue, that the trend is there. Peter asked me why. I am not certain, but this is my best current assessment: first, as I hinted at in my original answer, it probably has a lot to do with the fact that Government is much harder than it was 40 years ago. Ministers are under relentless public scrutiny in both the traditional and social media. The pressure to provide an immediate response to a problem or issue is enormous. Judgments about a Minister's competence are immediate and sometimes coruscating. Politics are rougher and less courteous. The Civil Service – still an essentially courteous environment, with its emphasis on looking at the evidence and weighing the options – sometimes struggles to meet expectations in this fast-moving world. It more often than previously gets caught in the crossfire.

Secondly, implementation – or 'delivery' – has also become more demanding and complex. Governments often bite off too much. Projects go wrong. The arguments about whether the Minister's original objectives or the civil servant's implementation are to blame for the failure can be tense. The temptation of Ministers is to put the blame on civil servants, who, they know, cannot answer back. There has certainly been a trend in the last seven years for more public criticism of, and briefing against, the Civil Service in general and individual civil servants in particular.

Thirdly, the explanation may lie partly in the changing nature of politicians themselves. In the last 20 years there have been more of two types of MP. First, there are those who are essentially managerial, sometimes as a result of what they have done outside Parliament. These often believe that they can manage the Civil Service better than the Civil Service itself, something that would almost never have been believed by MPs from either of the major parties 40 years ago. Clashes between Ministers and civil servants inevitably occur because of this more recent belief. Then there is a bigger and growing group of professional politicians who have done little else in their lives except inhabit the think tanks or been special advisers. They are intensely political, increasingly tribal and, in recent times, ideological. More of them are becoming Ministers – and, when they do, they are more likely than their predecessors to impose solutions worked out with a small group of other political advisers and allies. They are less interested in impartial advice, and sometimes not very interested in what civil servants think or say.]

Peter Hennessy

Our central theme is power, the notion of the power of Whitehall. It seems to me that the Civil Service is less powerful now than it was in your early days, not least because of the trust factor. But what about this new phenomenon of the rise of politically appointed special advisers to Ministers, and the multiplicity of think tanks? Both the special advisers and the think tanks provide increased sources of advice to politicians. I think it would be an exaggeration to say that the Civil Service had a monopoly on giving advice before the advent of these other, more partisan sources – but in terms of the geography of power, proximity to Ministers and the ability to get stuff in their red boxes (which contain all the papers a Minister has to attend to including correspondence, briefings and submissions), you were in pole position. You still are, but not to the same extent.

David Normington

I don't think that having a multiplicity of voices available to Ministers is bad for the development of policy as long as the Civil Service retains its distinctive voice, which is one of objectivity: looking at the evidence, providing the properly analysed policy advice. That is what the Civil Service can bring to the table. But I don't think it would be good for democracy if the Civil Service had a monopoly of advice. It never really did. Ministers have always taken external advice and been subject to the views of professional bodies, experts, businesses, trades unions and so on. Having lots of input from those who may be affected by a policy is essential to good policymaking.

Of course special advisers are in a special position because they work inside the system and have the ear of Ministers. They come in all shapes and sizes. On the one extreme some of them are almost like civil servants and just want to be policy wonks and on the other, some are very, very political indeed and really want to be Ministers. And then there's everyone in between. If Ministers didn't have special advisers, I would want to create them. There's a little group of special advisers that I wouldn't want to create, but on the whole special advisers are doing something that the Civil Service can't do. I have been in situations where my Minister didn't have a special adviser and needed political, not bureaucratic, advice. I have seen on those occasions the great temptation for the civil servants to step in and become political. That's a bad thing, and that's why special advisers are needed.

Peter Hennessy
Give us a quick character sketch of a special adviser who is a jolly good thing, and of one who is not.

David Normington
I've probably got a picture in my mind, though of course I won't put any names to it. I think a special adviser who is a good thing is one who sets out to work well with the Civil Service and secondly retains their distinctive political view. It's no good a special adviser becoming like a civil servant: you might just as well have civil servants. You want them to be distinctly political and to bring that sense of politics and Parliament to the table all the time, reminding the Minister how they got into power and what their manifesto says. That's what you want, but you want them to do it in constructive partnership.

The special adviser who is not a good thing is the one who sets out to have a battle with the Civil Service for the ear of the Minister, and when he or she has it, to do the Civil Service down. [During my career I have worked with some advisers, fortunately a minority, who deliberately created a barrier between the Minister and the Civil Service, who discouraged impartial, objective advice and deliberately undermined officials and, in some cases, other Ministers. That was rarely in the interests of the Minister and it certainly did not produce good policymaking.]

As in most walks of life, good Government needs good relationships between the key actors. When these are working, and when respectful, trusting relationships are preserved, Government works.

Peter Hennessy

What is the effect of greater publicity on civil servants? Has it recalibrated the balance of power? There were big changes in 1979 in the House of Commons, when for the first time we had a set of Select Committees of MPs of all parties that shadowed individual Departments. These meant that senior civil servants appeared far more frequently before Select Committees because there were many more of them. And also broadcasting, radio first and then television, meant that your profession came out of the cold. For some, it wasn't at all easy, but those who took to it naturally were regarded with deep suspicion in their Departments. You couldn't win. But do you not think that the nature of the governing partnership or marriage changed when civil servants came out through Parliament into the public?

David Normington

Well, it certainly became more difficult for civil servants. In front of Select Committees they have to navigate between being non-political, explaining and defending Government policy without indicating a political preference, but also being on the side of the Minister, not getting him or her into any trouble. It's difficult. I have had some torrid times in front of Select Committees. [One of my earliest in the Department of Education was to explain the failure of individual learning accounts, a programme which had led to the Government being defrauded of millions of pounds. Three months after I got to the Home Office I appeared before the Public Accounts Committee with my predecessor Permanent Secretary, explaining the alleged disappearance of foreign national prisoners and the Home Office's failure to produce satisfactory accounts.] Some of these encounters have been used since in training exercises in how to do it, but also how not to do it.

On balance, it's a good thing that civil servants have to defend the implementation of a policy; explaining policy is part of their role. On the whole, Government and democracy are better served by having civil servants explaining why and how they did things. But my 40 or 50 appearances before Select Committees and also the Public Accounts Committee over my time as a senior civil servant were tough, and I didn't always think at the time that it was good for Government or democracy! [The successful occasions were when a Committee was genuinely seeking to get to the facts of what had happened and why. I remember one Public Accounts Committee in particular when, for the first and only time, there was a genuine debate about the difficulties of controlling immigration and a real wish on the part of Committee members to understand why the tap could not simply be turned on and off. Unfortunately, that was all too rare. Too often it seemed to me that Committee members were playing a political game or seeking to humiliate the interviewee, often only with the aim of getting themselves into the media. The only effect of that is that the civil servant plays a game too, and is less forthcoming than he or she might have been. No one benefits.]

Peter Hennessy
Do you think the changes brought about by the 2000 Freedom of Information Act made things better or worse? It was another surge towards visibility and accountability, but of a different kind.

David Normington

Most people like me regret the Freedom of Information Act, because it has become more and more difficult to give advice in private to your Ministers. There are many things that can and should be put into the public domain, but the way in which the Act has developed has gradually encroached on that private space between politicians and civil servants. This hasn't helped their relationship, which as we have acknowledged is one of the most important aspects of good government. There has to be a safe time and space within which Ministers and civil servants can speak openly to each other and completely privately, so no one is worried about how it will look to the outside. I know most politicians who have been Ministers think that, and most civil servants think that, but the need for that space isn't well understood by the public, so they of course do not agree.

[I am not here talking about the vast amount of background evidence and information that the Civil Service provides as an aid to policy decisions. That should generally be in the public domain. I am simply referring to the advice that the civil servant offers to the Minister on a particular issue. If you want that advice to be frank, honest and objective, as the Civil Service Code requires, then there has to be scope for it to be offered in private and for the discussions that follow (and the minutes of the discussion) to remain private. Otherwise, civil servants will be less than frank and less and less will be written down (which is increasingly happening).]

Peter Hennessy

Do you think that the case for a politically neutral career Civil Service has to be remade anew in each Whitehall generation?

David Normington

Yes. I don't think we can ever take it for granted. We couldn't take it for granted in my last five years as Civil Service Commissioner, when I was responsible for senior appointments. The debates come and go but the concept of an impartial, non-politicised Civil Service is actually remarkably resilient. There's a common belief, particularly after long periods of one party in power, that civil servants will never be able to work for the new Government of a different party. But we always managed it – and managed it, I think, very successfully. However, the longer-term trend seems to be of a growing feeling that the non-political, impartial Civil Service is not serving Governments well enough. I don't think at this moment the non-political Civil Service is at risk, but I think there has been more of a political debate in the last five years about whether this model of a Civil Service which serves the present Government and the next, and provides objective advice, is the best model. I passionately believe it should be the model, but there have been increasing signs that there is less political acceptance of that than there used to be.

[Looking back now on my five years as First Civil Service Commissioner (between 2011 and 2016), it certainly felt as if the very nature of the Civil Service were being questioned as never before. The Government, mainly in the shape of the Minister responsible for the Civil Service, Francis Maude, grew increasingly vocal about the perceived inadequacy of the Service's senior leadership. Maude criticised individual senior civil servants, sought more Ministerial control over appointments and increasingly questioned the ethos and commitment of the Civil Service. He commissioned a study of other systems and showed serious interest in the Australian system, in which Ministers are supported by large political offices. In turn this encouraged a wider debate, in which a cross-party alliance of former Ministers set out proposals for how civil servants were appointed and for much greater political support for Ministers.

The paradox for civil servants is that, even when they are under this kind of sustained public questioning from their own Government or governing party, they cannot answer back publicly. Indeed, if it ever came to the point where a Government wanted to destroy the impartiality requirement, the Civil Service would be duty-bound to help the Government of the day to make that change.

That is why the Constitutional Reform and Governance Act 2010, which I talk about in my next answer, is so important. It enshrined the long-standing Civil Service conventions of impartiality and objectivity and appointment on merit in statute for the first time. It also gave statutory authority to the Civil Service Commission, meaning that I was the first Civil Service Commissioner in 155 years to have explicit Parliamentary authority for my role.

When Francis Maude and others questioned the enduring values of the Civil Service, therefore, I felt duty-bound to put across the counterarguments and to lead the Commission in resisting what seemed to us Government attempts to undermine Civil Service political impartiality. This didn't come easily for someone who had been a lifelong civil servant. But the fact is that I was no longer a civil servant. I was now a statutory office-holder, created by Parliament with a responsibility to protect the Civil Service values against anyone, including the Government of the day, who may be threatening them. That is what I did and would do again. It certainly did not make me popular with Francis Maude.]

Peter Hennessy
We live in an era now where a lot of what had been tacit has been written down. We have the Ministerial Code, which had been written down, of course, but as a Cabinet document called 'Questions and Procedure for Ministers'. Because it was a Cabinet document it had a 30-year 'classified' rule on it, so none but Ministers themselves knew the rule book for Ministers. Now the Ministerial Code is published, and there's the Civil Service Code, the Special Adviser Code, plus the new Cabinet Manual. Some have argued that this step has been very significant, moving these tacit understandings, these conventions at best, onto the face of a code. Is it a sign of the deterioration of these critical relationships between Ministers, civil servants and now special advisers too? In the old days, you could argue, you didn't have to write it down because everybody knew where the lines were. Clive Priestley from the Cabinet Office famously described it as the 'good chaps theory of Government' – good chaps of both sexes, of course. And the good chaps, both Ministers and officials, knew where the lines were and they didn't transgress them and there was a kind of built-in restraint which buttressed the confidence that you were talking about. So, it's a funny thing,

this codification. I'm actually in favour of it, I think it's necessary. We got to a point where it was necessary to start writing it down but in some ways it could be seen as a breakdown of the old relationships.

David Normington

I don't think codification and publication necessarily mean a breakdown of 'the old relationships'. I am always suspicious of looking back to a golden age, and I suspect there were lots of misunderstandings in the past. In my view, it is better to have roles and responsibilities written down because it leaves less room for doubt about respective roles. There are 150 years of wisdom distilled in the Civil Service Code [which is appended]. It's a remarkable document in my view. No doubt many civil servants rarely look at it, but if you want to and need to, it is a very brief, very clear, very compelling statement of what the Civil Service stands for. I think it's better for being written down.

But the most significant development in relation to the Civil Service of the last 30 years was the 2010 Constitutional Reform and Governance Act which put the Civil Service and indeed the Civil Service Commission and the values of the Civil Service into primary legislation. I used to think when I was a civil servant that didn't matter, partly because there were lots of good chaps, as Clive Priestley put it, in Parliament and in the Civil Service, who could be relied upon to behave themselves and understand the way the system works. But I've come to think, from the role I've had as First Civil Service Commissioner, that an impartial Civil Service needs the protection of primary legislation.

A non-politicised Civil Service: there's no inalienable right for it to exist – so I'd rather have it guaranteed by Parliament because then only Parliament can change it. That means that if we are going to change it we have to have a proper debate. The impartiality of the Civil Service can't now just be removed, as it could before, with the stroke of a pen in an Order in Council. [It is an extraordinary fact that for most of the last 150 years before 2010, the Civil Service has been governed by Orders in Council, that is to say, by executive powers exercised by Ministers through the Privy Council without recourse to Parliament.] If you are a politician, eager for all sorts of reasons, including laudable ones, to get policies through and delivered, it could be very tempting to remove a mode of working that introduces caution, slows things down and acts as a counterweight to your power. So it is helpful to all of us that the 2010 Act, which was passed by the skin of its teeth, just before the prorogation of Parliament, put the impartiality and political neutrality of the Civil Service into law.

Peter Hennessy
How significant are the new Extended Ministerial Offices? The idea, I think, is to have just under 20 people consisting of civil servants, special advisers and specialists. I think four Departments are working them up and they will have had to come to you for approval of the senior positions, I think, as First Commissioner. How significant are they? Should we worry about them as possibly a central directorate coming up in Departments which will marginalise the career officials, or do you think it's going with the grain?

David Normington
I think they are a really bad idea, but I don't know whether people understand what Extended Ministerial Offices are. As you describe them, they're a bit like 'cabinets'.

Peter Hennessy
French cabinets? Or Brussels?

David Normington
Even European 'cabinets'. For obvious reasons we can't describe them as *cabinets*, can we? But they are the idea that Ministers have around them a much larger office, and there goes with that the personal power of appointment. The convention has always been that Ministers delegate their powers of appointment to civil servants. In Extended Ministerial Offices, they do not. And that is a very significant change. However, as is often the way with our constitutional changes, they haven't made any difference yet. The first four Extended Ministerial Offices have not changed the mould. They look like slightly larger Private Offices of the traditional sort with special advisers and civil servants and one or two experts brought in, as has always happened. So, it hasn't changed the world yet, but these things could be on a long timescale.

I think there are these two risks: One is that it blurs the concept of an impartial civil servant appointed on merit, by allowing Ministers to choose people to be civil servants without competition; that changes the nature of the Civil Service fundamentally and is certainly against the spirit, if not the letter, of the 2010 Act. The other risk is that it creates a big office around the Minister, with the Civil Service at a distance. The model is – you see it in Australia, in fact – that Ministers have dozens of quasi-political appointees around them, often in a different city from the Civil Service.

[The Extended Ministerial Office was the brainchild of Francis Maude and the clearest example of the Coalition Government's wish to change the nature of the Civil Service. It caused the Civil Service Commission major concern and we used our powers under the 2010 Act to neutralise, as far as we could, the risks of politicising the Civil Service. This included a prohibition on appointees who were recruited by the Minister personally, without open competition, from joining the mainstream Civil Service without undergoing a further fair and open competition. As it turned out, we need not have worried too much, since one of Theresa May's first acts, when she became Prime Minister, was to abolish Extended Ministerial Offices. Some believe that was because she was a strong proponent of the traditional values of the Civil Service. The more cynical argue that she – or rather her special advisers – did not welcome the idea of other Cabinet Ministers having large political offices, in effect creating alternative power bases to her own at 10 Downing Street. Much more recently, Extended Ministerial Offices are making a reappearance in the form of policy advisers to Secretaries of State, but with the important condition that they, like the rest of the Civil Service, are selected by civil servants on merit.]

Peter Hennessy
How crucial is the idea of a unified Civil Service for the whole of the UK? We've had it since time immemorial, but how sustainable is it, do you think, given the 'devo max' to

Scotland, and what I fear could be a creeping estrangement between Scotland and Westminster/Whitehall even if the countries don't separate?

David Normington

I think you and I probably share a deep commitment to the Union, don't we?

Peter Hennessy

We do, we do.

David Normington

So, my answer really comes from that commitment. I think a unified Civil Service is an essential part of the glue of the UK and, more particularly, I think that the enduring values of the Civil Service are part of that glue. I think it is very, very important that we maintain a Civil Service which shares the same understandings, the same approaches and the same values all across the UK. Of course, if Scotland gains independence, the Civil Service will break up, but until then I think it's a good thing to have a unified Civil Service.

Peter Hennessy

Is it fraying a bit? Is that glue weakening?

David Normington

It's fraying in the sense that it is hard to get people in London to take enough interest in Scotland. The Civil Service has to work at the glue; it doesn't keep its strength to bind us together without an effort. If you're Scottish and a civil servant it's much more interesting these days to be in Scotland [because of the increasing powers and influence of the Scottish Government. That means many fewer Scots work in the Civil Service in London than when I started out. In consequence, fewer UK civil servants understand Scotland, and fewer Scottish civil servants understand Whitehall]. So, I think there's a lot to be worked at.

I can tell you a story, however, that should give us hope. The rule for appointments of Permanent Secretaries now is that the Prime Minister, and in Scotland the First Minister, chooses from a list of appointable candidates drawn up by the Civil Service Commission. While I was First Commissioner, we appointed the Permanent Secretary in Scotland. So, the appointment was organised by the UK Civil Service Commission under the Commission's rules but, since she was the final decision-taker, I had a lot of dealings with the First Minister over it. As I was reassuring her on the Scottish credentials of the appointable candidates, the First Minister said, 'David, they need to be good, that's what matters, they need to be good.' So, appointment on merit is alive and well in Scotland, as in England and Wales.

Peter Hennessy
Do you have a sense, David, of the importance of the notion of Crown service to the Civil Service? It is very important to the Armed Forces – the Navy, Army and Air Force – because the Queen is Commander-in-Chief and their members swear allegiance to her. The balance of power that creates would help prevent any attempt by an elected Government to become a tyranny. And the same is true of the Secret Services of MI5,

MI6 and GCHQ. In some intangible way, they cherish the notion of Crown service, and it seems to me the notion is more powerful in the secret world and in the Armed Forces than perhaps it is in the Civil Service.

David Normington

I think you're right. Civil servants don't talk so much about being Crown servants any more. It's a pity, really, because the connection of the Civil Service with the non-partisan part of the constitution actually expresses very clearly that the Civil Service serves the Government of the day through the Crown. I think there's something really powerful there. Maybe the Home civil servants here should refresh their thinking about that. The Armed Forces and the Security Services prize it so much, I think, because they so deeply value their independent and non-political status. It should perhaps be the same for the Civil Service.

Peter Hennessy

Can you give us a swift audit of your hopes and fears about public service? Hopes first.

David Normington

The Civil Service remains a place of remarkable people, remarkable skills and remarkable resilience. We're very, very lucky to have it. In the last six years we have lost 80,000 jobs in the Home Civil Service, not to mention cuts in the Diplomatic Service. We've hardly given anybody a pay rise. There's been a lot of public debate about poor performance and public criticism of the kind we have talked about. Yet the

Civil Service goes on doing the job in the very best way it can, for the benefit of the public. We must not take it for granted or let it fall into disrepair through neglect and underinvestment. It's hard, though, to get people to speak up for the Civil Service very much, because people aren't really interested in it or don't even know very much about it. I sometimes think that the Civil Service doesn't stand up for itself enough but, of course, for reasons I have explained, that is not really possible.

At the same time we must also continue to make it as good as it can be, improving the leadership, updating skills, investing in digital technology, making it more efficient. I am not making a plea here for the status quo. We have to go on changing and updating to meet the new challenges. The greatest risk of all to the Civil Service is that it doesn't do a good job, thus creating the opportunity to say 'it's not doing a good job, so let's try some other model'. The perfect model is a skilled, efficient Civil Service, open to change but rooted in its traditional values of impartiality and political neutrality. But we're very lucky to have it. I guess I would say that after 40 years' service!

Peter Hennessy

Your independence gives you moral agency as a civil servant, even though you have to follow the direction set by Ministers. You have to ensure the direction is within the law and bound by propriety, and if you cannot do that, your nuclear weapon is resignation. What would have triggered your resignation?

David Normington

As First Civil Service Commissioner? If the Government

decided to make an appointment of someone as Permanent Secretary or other senior Civil Service post whom we had said was not suitable and was not on merit appointable: that would have been a resigning matter for me and the whole Commission. Perhaps because the Government knows that, it never got to that stage.

Peter Hennessy
Have you ever considered resigning in your previous roles in the Civil Service?

David Normington
No. And if I had, I wouldn't tell you in this public forum! I've had my ups and downs, of course, but I think it's better to stay and stand up for what you think is right if you possibly can. And, of course, a lot of damage can be done in the resignation itself. After 42 years I know that taking on the Government by issuing resignation threats is a mug's game for people in our sort of roles because you always end up losing. [The party machines can be totally ruthless in turning on a civil servant who has decided to resign on a point of principle. In any battle between a Minister and civil servant, it will be rare for the civil servant to win the media battle, even if he or she has right on their side.

The nearest I came to resigning was in 2006 when I was Permanent Secretary at the Home Office. John Reid became Home Secretary and declared the Home Office 'not fit for purpose'. Initially he and I simply did not see eye to eye. He rarely sought my advice, did not value my opinion and made it pretty clear that he did not believe I could put the Home

Office back on its feet. I had always believed that, if relations between a Permanent Secretary and Secretary of State were irretrievably broken, then it served no one's purpose for the Permanent Secretary to remain in post. It was largely my wife who persuaded me to stay and prove John Reid wrong. That is effectively what I did. The Home Office recovered from its meltdown. Our mutual respect slowly grew. While we did not agree on everything – and particularly not on his wish to break up the Home Office – we were in due course able to talk things over and resolve our differences. When he resigned from the Government, we parted on good terms.

It is always likely to be these failures of personal relationships, not policy differences, which bring a civil servant to the point of resignation. Civil servants have a high tolerance of policies they do not agree with or of having their advice ignored. As I have explained, it is in the DNA of a civil servant that he or she may have to implement policies they deeply disagree with. If you can't live with that, you are probably not cut out to be a civil servant.

There are also important safety valves in the system. If, for example, you have a moral or ethical objection to a policy, it is understood that you can ask to be moved from that policy area. If you feel that you are being asked to do something improper or unlawful – and in the unlikely event that you cannot dissuade your Secretary of State – there are well-established procedures for informing the Cabinet Secretary or Prime Minister, or in some cases the First Civil Service Commissioner. Finally, where a Permanent Secretary believes that a policy represents a poor use or misuse of public money, he or she may seek a formal direction that the Secretary of State intends to go ahead nevertheless and will account directly to Parliament for his decision.]

Peter Hennessy
If you were graduating this summer, would you put in for the Civil Service again?

David Normington
Oh yes, definitely. I would be clearer now, of course, than I was in 1973 that it was a great place to work. You don't go into the Civil Service for the monetary rewards, but the compensations are: fascinating work; insight – if you're in Whitehall itself – into politics; and the ability to do something worthwhile, something for the public. All those things are amazing – I mean absolutely amazing – even though there are things in my career that haven't gone so well. When I've been pretty unhappy, mostly it's been worth it. [When I see educational standards rising because of an education policy I have worked on; or an Employment Act for which I led the Bill team still on the statute book and doing good, 38 years after its passage through Parliament; or the country safer because of measures to improve the effectiveness of the country's counterterrorism response; and much more, I look back with satisfaction that I played my part and the country is better for it.]

Peter Hennessy
Well, David, you've given us a fascinating set of insights into the power of Whitehall. Thank you very much indeed.

A Brexit Postscript

by David Normington

Just over six months after this dialogue, the British people voted by 52% to 48% to leave the European Union. The vote to leave was a profound shock for Whitehall, as it was for the whole political establishment. The Civil Service suddenly found itself faced with the implementation of a decision which it did not expect, had not prepared for (indeed had been forbidden by the Prime Minister from doing so) and did not want. Former Prime Minister David Cameron said it was 'the most complex and most important task that the British Civil Service has undertaken in decades'. In my view, it is the greatest challenge it has faced outside wartime.

As I have watched from outside the Civil Service since the result, I have been immensely proud of my former colleagues. Within days of the referendum they picked themselves up, started to understand the enormity of the task and readied themselves to support the incoming Government of a new Prime Minister. In doing so they gave the most vivid illustration of the importance of a professional Civil Service rooted in the values of impartiality and objectivity.

I have never worried that the Civil Service is too pro-EU to undertake the task. As we discussed in the dialogue, it is deep in the culture to serve the Government of the day with dedication and commitment. Even among those who still believe that Brexit is a profound mistake, there are many who are energised by the challenge and determined to prove that the exit can be achieved with skill and professionalism. We are lucky at this moment to have a non-political Civil Service. Imagine if we were attempting this task having replaced the top three layers of the administration because the Government had changed, or if the only people counselling the Government were political advisers identified with one or other of the two sides of the argument? The former Cabinet Secretary Lord Butler has argued that Brexit may result in a resurgence of the Civil Service because Ministers will once again come to rely on, and value, the professionalism of impartial civil servants.

I hope he is right, but there are dangers as well.

One risk is the sheer enormity of the task. As I described in the dialogue, the Civil Service has been hollowed out by the years of austerity; there is a scramble to reverse some of the 80,000 job losses. There is a danger that the whole administration of Government will be overwhelmed by the breadth and complexity of the task. The process of implementation is likely to take years to complete, during which time the public and politicians will be bored with the painstaking detail and want to move on. Even if the negotiations can be successfully concluded on time, there is then the huge administrative and legal burden of changing our regulations, institutions and systems – for immigration, for example, or customs, or agricultural subsidies, or fisheries or a hundred other areas – which affect people's lives. The scope for systems not changing in time, or for those affected not understanding the new rules or for things just getting missed or forgotten is very real. In such cases the temptation to blame the Civil Service will be too great to resist.

Secondly, the Civil Service can only do the detailed work on exit if there is a clear political lead on what Brexit means in the key policy areas. It can advise on the options but it cannot and must not fill the void itself. Unfortunately, the Government has been slow to resolve its internal differences and, even when the fog begins to lift, there is the added complication of a fragile majority in Parliament. People often used to joke that civil servants liked nothing better than a weak Government because they could get on and do what they liked. But the opposite is true. There is nothing the Civil Service likes less than a Minister or, worse, a whole Government, which does not know its own mind. Usually in those circumstances it muddles through until the Government or Minister moves on. But muddling through the exit from the EU is not really an option.

Thirdly, the tensions between civil servants and politicians, which we discussed in the dialogue, bubble not far beneath the surface. There continue to be politicians, mainly the passionate Brexiteers, who think it should be relatively easy to withdraw from the EU. They find facts and detail frustrating, and blame the civil servants for putting negatives and difficulties in the way. There have been public accusations from politicians, and even from a Government Minister, that the Civil Service is deliberately seeking to thwart the withdrawal by exaggerating the difficulties and distorting the analysis. Fortunately, the reaction against these politicians has been swift and critical and has done more damage to them than to the Civil Service. Given the passions which Brexit continues to stir – and the different perspectives and roles of politicians and civil servants – it is inevitable that these skirmishes will continue to arise.

Civil servants are, of course, not paragons of virtue, but human beings. There may well be some who are tempted to labour over the difficulties or to emphasise the negatives, rather than offer solutions. As discussed in the dialogue, it is no easy job in normal times to find the right way of speaking truth to power. Against the heightened tensions of Brexit, it is even more difficult to bring forth inconvenient evidence or genuinely bad news without being accused of seeking to delay the process of exit. However, I have no doubt that the commitment of the Civil Service as a whole to support the Government of the day is as strong as ever, and that the leadership of the Civil Service will ensure that, unless and until there is a different political instruction, Brexit is delivered to the best of their ability. There is no possibility of a Civil Service conspiracy to thwart Brexit. That is simply not in its DNA.

Finally, there is a more profound issue here. I have always believed – and it underpinned many of my answers to Peter Hennessy's questions – that we have a system of Government which is resilient to whatever is thrown at it and that good, effective politicians, supported by high-quality civil servants, rooted in parliamentary democracy, would see us through the toughest times. Now, in the aftermath of the referendum and the subsequent election, I am not so sure.

The referendum was not simply a vote against the EU. A substantial section of the public used it to reject the advice of their elected representatives; to protest about what they saw as years of neglect of their families and communities; and to show that they did not trust the Westminster and Whitehall establishment to act in their best interests.

What sustained me over 42 years of public service was the belief that the Civil Service exists to serve the public good by enacting the will of the democratically elected Government of the day. That remains the guiding star of most civil servants and the reason they get up each day to go to work. But it is not so easy, post-referendum, to discern the will of the British people or, for that matter, of the democratically elected Government. The referendum showed that the country was split almost 50/50 on what is in its best interests. There is little sign that many people have changed their minds since. A weakened Government has struggled to define a way forward which commands majority support in the country: it may not win support for its final deal in Parliament. MPs themselves, with a few notable exceptions, have seemed delegitimised by the referendum result, seemingly bound to obey a result with which many fundamentally disagree. This is a crisis for democratic government – not just for politicians and Parliament but, since government is a joint endeavour, for the Civil Service too. Whatever the future for Brexit – hard, soft, somewhere in between or not at all – the priority for politicians and civil servants must be not just to negotiate a successful future for the UK, but to restore public trust in the way the country is run.

Notes

1 Stafford H. Northcote and C.E. Trevelyan, *Report on the Organisation of the Permanent Civil Service* (London, HMSO, 1854).

2 Ibid., p. 3.

3 Ibid., p. 4.

4 Ibid., p. 22.

5 Claire Foster-Gilbert, *The Moral Heart of Public Service* (London, JKP, 2017), p. 61.

6 Martin Donnelly, 'Positive Neutrality and Trust: the policy role of a permanent civil service', Speech given for the Foreign and Commonwealth Office, 16th October 2014, p. 5.

7 Peter Waller, *Understanding Whitehall: a short introduction for special advisers* (The Constitution Unit, University College, London, 2014), p. 21.

8 Ibid., p. 5.

9 Donnelly, op. cit., p. 11.

10 Clare Moriarty, 'Values and Value Conflict in the Civil Service' (London, Department for Transport, 2006).

The Civil Service Code

Civil Service values

The statutory basis for the management of the Civil Service is set out in Part 1 of the Constitutional Reform and Governance Act 2010.

The Civil Service is an integral and key part of the Government of the United Kingdom.[1] It supports the Government of the day in developing and implementing its policies, and in delivering public services. Civil servants are accountable to Ministers,[2] who in turn are accountable to Parliament.[3]

As a civil servant, you are appointed on merit on the basis of fair and open competition and are expected to carry out your role with dedication and a commitment to the Civil Service and its core values: integrity, honesty, objectivity and impartiality.

In this Code:

- 'integrity' is putting the obligations of public service above your own personal interests
- 'honesty' is being truthful and open
- 'objectivity' is basing your advice and decisions on rigorous analysis of the evidence
- 'impartiality' is acting solely according to the merits of the case and serving equally well Governments of different political persuasions

These core values support good government and ensure the achievement of the highest possible standards in all that the Civil Service does. This in turn helps the Civil Service to gain and retain the respect of Ministers, Parliament, the public and its customers.

This Code[4] sets out the standards of behaviour expected of you and other civil servants. These are based on the core values which are set out in legislation. Individual Departments may also have their own separate mission and values statements based on the core values, including the standards of behaviour expected of you when you deal with your colleagues.

Standards of behaviour
Integrity
You must:

- fulfil your duties and obligations responsibly
- always act in a way that is professional[5] and that deserves and retains the confidence of all those with whom you have dealings[6]
- carry out your fiduciary obligations responsibly (that is make sure public money and other resources are used properly and efficiently)
- deal with the public and their affairs fairly, efficiently, promptly, effectively and sensitively, to the best of your ability
- ensure you have ministerial authorisation for any contact with the media[7]
- keep accurate official records and handle

information as openly as possible within the legal framework

- comply with the law and uphold the administration of justice

You must not:

- misuse your official position, for example by using information acquired in the course of your official duties to further your private interests or those of others
- accept gifts or hospitality or receive other benefits from anyone which might reasonably be seen to compromise your personal judgement or integrity
- disclose official information without authority (this duty continues to apply after you leave the Civil Service)

Honesty
You must:

- set out the facts and relevant issues truthfully, and correct any errors as soon as possible
- use resources only for the authorised public purposes for which they are provided

You must not:

- deceive or knowingly mislead Ministers, Parliament or others

- be influenced by improper pressures from others or the prospect of personal gain

Objectivity

You must:

- provide information and advice, including advice to Ministers, on the basis of the evidence, and accurately present the options and facts
- take decisions on the merits of the case
- take due account of expert and professional advice

You must not:

- ignore inconvenient facts or relevant considerations when providing advice or making decisions
- frustrate the implementation of policies once decisions are taken by declining to take, or abstaining from, action which flows from those decisions

Impartiality

You must:

- carry out your responsibilities in a way that is fair, just and equitable and reflects the Civil Service commitment to equality and diversity

You must not:

- act in a way that unjustifiably favours or discriminates against particular individuals or interests

Political impartiality
You must:

- serve the Government,[2] whatever its political persuasion, to the best of your ability in a way which maintains political impartiality and is in line with the requirements of this Code, no matter what your own political beliefs are
- act in a way which deserves and retains the confidence of Ministers, while at the same time ensuring that you will be able to establish the same relationship with those whom you may be required to serve in some future Government
- comply with any restrictions that have been laid down on your political activities

You must not:

- act in a way that is determined by party political considerations, or use official resources for party political purposes
- allow your personal political views to determine any advice you give or your actions

Rights and responsibilities
Your Department or Agency has a duty to make you aware

of this Code and its values. If you believe that you are being required to act in a way which conflicts with this Code, your Department or Agency must consider your concern, and make sure that you are not penalised for raising it.

If you have a concern, you should start by talking to your line manager or someone else in your line management chain. If for any reason you would find this difficult, you should raise the matter with your Department's nominated officers who have been appointed to advise staff on the Code. If you become aware of actions by others which you believe conflict with this Code you should report this to your line manager or someone else in your line management chain; alternatively you may wish to seek advice from your nominated officer. You should report evidence of criminal or unlawful activity to the police or other appropriate regulatory authorities. This Code does not cover HR management issues.

If you have raised a matter in accordance with the relevant procedures,[7] and do not receive what you consider to be a reasonable response, you may report the matter to the Civil Service Commission.[8] The Commission will also consider taking a complaint direct.

If the matter cannot be resolved using the procedures set out above, and you feel you cannot carry out the instructions you have been given, you will have to resign from the Civil Service.

This Code is part of the contractual relationship between you and your employer. It sets out the high standards of behaviour expected of you which follow from your position in public and national life as a civil servant. You can take pride in living up to these values.

Notes

1   Civil servants working for the Scottish and Welsh
     Governments, and their Agencies, have their own
     versions of the Code. Similar codes apply to the
     Northern Ireland Civil Service and the Diplomatic
     Service. Civil servants working in non-ministerial
     Departments in England, Scotland and Wales are
     covered by this Code.

2   Some civil servants are accountable to the office-holder
     in charge of their organisation. This is made clear in
     terms and conditions of employment.

3   Civil servants advising Ministers should be aware of
     the constitutional significance of Parliament, and of
     the conventions governing the relationship between
     Parliament and the Government.

4   The respective responsibilities placed on Ministers
     and special advisers in relation to the Civil Service
     are set out in their codes of conduct. Special advisers
     are also covered by this Civil Service Code except, in
     recognition of their specific role, the requirements for
     objectivity and impartiality.

5   Including taking account of ethical standards governing
     particular professions.

6   Including a particular recognition of the importance of
     co-operation and mutual respect between civil servants
     working for the UK Government and the devolved
     administrations and vice versa.

7   The whistleblowing legislation (the Public Interest
     Disclosure Act 1998) may also apply in some
     circumstances. The 'Directory of Civil Service

Guidance' and the 'Civil Service Management Code' give more information.

8   The Civil Service Commission's 'Guide to bringing a complaint' gives more information. It is available on the Civil Service Commission website.

Westminster Abbey Institute

The Power of Civil Servants is published in partnership with Westminster Abbey Institute. Westminster Abbey Institute was established in 2013 to nurture and revitalise moral and spiritual values in public life, inspire the vocation to public service in those working in Westminster and Whitehall, identify and defend what is morally healthy in their institutions and promote wider understanding of public service. The Institute draws on Westminster Abbey's resources of spirituality and scholarship, rooted in its Christian tradition and long history as a place of quiet reflection on Parliament Square.